"If you want valuable guidance on how to succeed in business and, more importantly, how to succeed in life, then Life with Flavor *is a must read. Meet Jim Herr and learn. And whatever you do, do NOT skip Mim's Notes in the Epilogue!"*

President George H. W. Bush

∽∾

"It's more than a blueprint for a delicious chip and successful business. Jim's words offer an inspiring recipe for a fulfilling life of faith, family and community."

Governor Tom Ridge, Former Governor of Pennsylvania
First Secretary, U.S. Department of Homeland Security

∽∾

"One of the great blessings of ministry is meeting people that exemplify living life to its fullest. Jim Herr is such a man. So it is fitting that he entitled his new book Life with Flavor. *For those who have family businesses or have a desire to start a business, or for those who just want to be inspired by a story of turning hardships into victories or heartaches into blessings, this book is for you. Jim Herr and his entire family have a story that will touch hearts as accounts are given to what the Lord will do in lives that are committed to Him. Many dream of spicing up their lives. I encourage readers to consider how Jim Herr found favor with God and how his faithfulness to God's Word flavored his life."*

Franklin Graham, President and CEO
Billy Graham Evangelistic Association and Samaritan's Purse

"My wife and I sought the advice and counsel of Jim and Mim Herr around their breakfast table before I first ran for public office.

Their life story is both inspiring and instructional on not only how to build a successful business but how to live a productive life. Young entrepreneurs and small businesses would do well to emulate their example of ethical stewardship and good judgment.

This is a short book full of lessons learned from a life well-lived."

Congressman Joseph R. Pitts
16th Congressional District, Pennsylvania

∽o∾

"The world is a beautiful place when nice guys finish first. James Stauffer Herr is one of the nicest people in the world. Jim's story personifies the American dream that hard work, perseverance and an entrepreneurial spirit are the ingredients for success.

I have known Jim for close to 40 years. Our company became a customer of Herr's shortly after opening our first store on April 16th, 1964. Over this period Herr's has often been rated by our store managers as providing the best service of all Direct Store Delivery vendors and is consistently rated in the top 10%. While the business success of Herr's is much to be admired, the relationship of their family to the business and to each other is equally remarkable. Most family businesses fall on hard times in the 2nd or 3rd generation; Herr's is built to last because of the values that Jim and Mim have instilled in their family. If you like stories of people with a passion for the Lord, a desire to help others and a happy ending, read Life with Flavor!*"*

Dick Wood, Chairman, Wawa

"As I read the book Life with Flavor, this thought keeps recurring: Jim and his Lady, Mim, reflect the life of their Lord, who was filled "with grace and truth." Sometimes, people who major on graciousness fudge on the truth, and people who major on truth can be brittle and even unkind.

In this compelling volume you read the story of a man who, without trimming his stated convictions, built a world class business. I have traveled around the world with Jim and Mim, and they live out their "grace and truth" commitment 24/7. May God give this book wide broadcast."

John Haggai, Founder and Chairman, Haggai Institute

∽◇∾

"What a wonderful book! No one better demonstrates all that has made our country great than Jim Herr. He created a successful business by following the principles of honesty, humility, integrity and old fashioned hard work... all guided by a strong faith.

There are no better examples for all of us to be successful in business and in life than those in this book. Jim Herr's wisdom and experience is a great gift to anyone who reads Life with Flavor."

Dan Danner, President
National Federation of Independent Business

∽◇∾

"Over the years the Phillies have enjoyed teaming up with another Philly favorite, Herr's Snack Foods. Jim's book contains the details of hits, homeruns and a few errors in the company he founded."

Bill Giles, Chairman, Philadelphia Phillies

"I would like to offer the appreciation of the entire snack food industry to Mr. James S. Herr for his leadership and devotion to the Snack Food Association and the industry he helped build. He has always believed that the association's principle duty is to ensure that our industry is well represented in the corridors of government so that the entrepreneurial spirit that made our industry strong is not forgotten.

I want to congratulate Jim Herr on this autobiography of his great life and work. In short, Jim is a highly respected businessman who created his successful company through honest hard work, devotion to family, dedication to his country and a strong belief in God. The snack industry will always be grateful to Jim Herr for sharing his wisdom and great talents in building our association and industry."

James McCarthy, President and CEO
Snack Food Association

Life with Flavor

A Personal History of Herr's

James S. Herr, Founder

with Bruce E. Mowday

and June Herr Gunden

Fort Lee, New Jersey

BARRICADE BOOKS

Published by Barricade Books, Fort Lee, New Jersey

Copyright © 2012 by Herr Foods Inc.

PRINTED IN THE UNITED STATES OF AMERICA
By DavCo Advertising, Inc., Kinzers, Pennsylvania

Cover Design by Herr Foods Design Team
Text Design by Anita W. Taylor
Editorial Services by Peachtree Editorial Service, Peachtree City, Georgia
Pictures from Herr's 65th Anniversary DVD Courtesy of AVIO Productions

ISBN 13 9781569804698
ISBN 10 1569804699

Library of Congress Cataloging-in-Publication Data
Herr, James Stauffer, 1924-2012
  Life with Flavor! : A Personal History of Herr's / by James S. Herr with
  Bruce E. Mowday and June Herr Gunden.
    p. cm.
  Includes bibliographical references.
  ISBN 978-1-56980-469-8
  1. Herr, James Stauffer, 1924- 2012. Herr family. 3. Herr Foods (Firm)–History.
  4. Businesspeople–United States–Biography. 5. Food industry and trade–United
  States. I. Mowday, Bruce. II. Gunden, June.
  III. Title.
   HD9000.9.U5H397 2012
   338.7'6646--dc23
                    2012012371

Second printing

Printed on acid free paper.

Dedicated to the memory of James S. Herr,

the founder and inspiration of Herr Foods Inc.,

who died April 5, 2012,

after the manuscript was completed.

This posthumous autobiography honors the career

and life of a remarkable man.

TABLE OF CONTENTS

ACKNOWLEDGMENTS

Just as our business was built by the efforts of many, this book came about through many people. I am actually not the writer, but I am the author of the content, in that it records my thoughts and my life's message.

The research has come from Bruce E. Mowday, who interviewed many of our family members, employees, and associates, and he compiled a draft of the material. It was then re-shaped and put into my words by my daughter June and her husband, Doug, who have a business that provides editorial services. From there, other members of our family fine-tuned it, so it is truly a joint effort.

I thank all who gave of their memories and their efforts to make this book possible.

James S. Herr

INTRODUCTION

Many people like the idea of building something from nothing. In business, the one who builds an enterprise from scratch is called an entrepreneur, and that's how I'm often labeled.

I didn't necessarily set out to become an entrepreneur—I didn't even know that was an option—but perhaps the idea appeals to you. Perhaps you would like to start a business or expand an enterprise and you wonder, "How could I do that? Could you give me any tips?"

Whatever I have learned along the way I will be happy to share with you. As I tell my story, I'll summarize some key principles that you may find helpful. I would like to encourage you to accomplish all that you personally were created to do, because that's when you truly live life with zest and purpose—with *flavor*.

I believe the Great Creator is the model entrepreneur. Starting from nothing, He made the whole world! Afterwards, the Bible says, He made human beings "in His own image." He made us to be creative and to work hard at something, just like He did. That's why I think we instinctively admire these values.

The book of Proverbs has greatly influenced my thinking as a business person. Throughout my story I will share some of the practical words of advice in it, as they relate to decisions or situations I've faced (they are taken from *Living Psalms and Proverbs*, by Dr. Kenneth Taylor).

I hope that something I say will spark that inborn gift God created within you, so that you can be encouraged in your life's work and live life with flavor!

Prologue

HERR FOODS TODAY

First I'll tell you a little bit about Herr's today.

The main products we sell are potato chips, pretzels, popcorn, cheese curls, tortilla chips, pork rinds, crackers, and nuts. We manufacture about 85 percent of these products. Our stated mission is to increase sales profitably by safely providing the best products and service available.

If you live in our area of the country (the mid-Atlantic, Greater Philadelphia region) you may be familiar with our turquoise, red, and white route sales trucks. They are one of our best assets because of the relationships and the service they represent. Local store managers want to buy products from someone who knows and cares about their business and personally delivers fresh products. The Herr's salesperson keeps the store's shelves stocked and introduces the manager to our new products, which contributes to the store's success. Today we have more than 500 routes operating from 20 warehouses and two plants, and I think the best way to learn about what Herr's is all about is to operate one of those routes. That is the "ground floor" of our operation.

Of course, Herr's gets calls all the time from other areas of the country, and we want to grow, so we have developed other methods of sales. One is national sales, where our sales people work with retailers who have chain stores nationwide. This is a growing part of our business, and we hope that in the future we will become much more well-known across our country. Our export business is also growing rapidly, so maybe you'll see our product when you travel overseas.

Right now we have about 1,500 employees. We work hard to maintain healthy relationships and two-way communication, and I'm pleased that there are no unions involved. To me that would be an indication that our management team is not doing a good job of fostering our culture of being "one family" of people, striving together to build a better company. Our goal is to continue that culture, which I believe explains why we have so many long-term employees.

In 2013, Herr Foods Inc., with annual sales of over $250 million, ranked in the top five of independently-owned salty snack food companies in the country.

But Herr's today is very different from anything I anticipated as a young man. Let me tell you a little about my early life.

Jim as a teenager on his dad's farm

Chapter 1

I KNEW WHAT I *DIDN'T* WANT TO DO

I was born on August 6, 1924, and raised in the village of Willow Street, Pennsylvania, a farming community south of Lancaster. I was the second child born to Ira L. and Mary Stauffer Herr. (My middle name is Stauffer, after Mom's maiden name.) There were five children in my family: Christian, me, Mary, Ira, and Anna Mae.

My father purchased our 86-acre farm in 1925 for $5,000. During my early childhood our nation was going through the Great Depression. My dad would often remind us, "Don't spread the butter too thick." You could make the butter last by not using a lot at one time. It was a time to be frugal, very frugal. I'm not saying we suffered when we were spreading the butter thin. Since we were farmers, we had enough to eat and we did not experience some of the ravaging effects of the Depression that others in our country suffered. But we were very careful about how we earned and spent money.

My perception was that we were poor compared to some of my buddies' families. Their dads' farms seemed to have plenty of tractors and cars. Whenever my family got a car, it would already be five years old or so. We didn't have a tractor until I was a teenager and then we got a used Fordson row crop tractor. I used to plow with mules, not horses, before we got the Fordson.

My father was a conservative man. He believed that all of his children should work on the farm until we were 21 years old and then we could decide what career we wanted to pursue. Before that time, if we made money in some other way, such as doing a task for a neighbor, we were expected to give the money to our parents to be used for family expenses.

"Pop" also believed the boys should be given a car for working on the farm. (The girls were given comparable money toward household items.) One of the most important times for a boy was when he turned 16 and was able to drive a car. Having driven the farm vehicles, I knew how to drive before I was 16. But I didn't get my first car—a used 1940 Olds Cruiser—until I was 19 years old.

My childhood was nurtured by working with my family on the farm, spending time with our large extended family, and attending regular worship services at Willow Street Mennonite Church. Our heritage in the Mennonite church was a huge factor in how our family lived our lives. In fact, I'll share with you a little bit more about Mennonites, to help you understand why we thought the way we did.

Mennonites are Protestants who are traditionally pacifists and choose options other than the military to serve our country. We are known for traits like humility, thriftiness, and concern for others (especially in areas such as disaster relief). At the time I grew up there was also a major emphasis on living a simple way of life, shunning materialism, and being separate from the values of the surrounding culture (the "world"). In our area, being separate meant that we dressed differently from others—you could easily tell who was a Mennonite and who wasn't. We were encouraged to stay separate, to be "plain" and not "worldly," and not to engage too much in the larger culture in such ways as voting in elections.

Some people link us to the Amish, but the Amish are a completely different group. Unlike them, Mennonites do not object to modern conveniences and transportation methods. No longer do most Mennonites live on the farm and stay as separate from the larger culture as the Amish do. And the people in our family do not dress differently any more, though some Mennonite groups still do.

At the time I was growing up, my family valued hard work above formal education. Perhaps my parents were afraid that education would cause their children to stray from the simple way of life and to become more like the "world," rather than staying separated from it. My father did not think it was necessary for us to go to high school, and he felt he needed us to help on the farm; accordingly, after I began the ninth grade, he encouraged me to quit school. Though I enjoyed school, and I especially loved to play basketball there, I went along with my father's wishes. I trusted that he knew what was best for me, and it was gratifying to know I was needed and that I was old enough to do a man's job.

Each child on the Herr farm was responsible for a specific area of work, though of course we all had to help wherever we were needed. My special job was to take care of the poultry operation, a task I

Tobacco Shed, early site of Herr's Potato Chips

Herr Farm, Willow Street, PA

came to dislike, because there was no one to talk to all day long but chickens! We had about 2,000 laying hens at the time, and I had to clean the eggs. My brothers took care of our herd of cows, which numbered eleven or twelve.

We also grew a number of crops on the farm, such as corn, soybeans, wheat, and grass for the hay. We grew tobacco at one time, but eventually we stopped, mostly as a matter of conscience. My parents didn't approve of smoking, so even though growing tobacco was lucrative, they decided we shouldn't be growing it. We changed to tomatoes instead, and we sold our crop to Campbell's for making soup.

A typical day for me began about 5:00 A.M. I would help do the milking and then eat breakfast, before starting the rest of the daily farm chores. This was pretty much the norm for all of us and we didn't think it was unusual to work long days, especially when the crops or herds demanded it.

Some of the good times I remember centered on going to farm shows, local fairs, and family gatherings. I especially enjoyed playing ball with cousins and neighbors. As a teenager I decided I wanted to play the guitar and found a good local teacher, Howard Simmons. He had an "orchestra" of stringed instruments that would perform here and there and I loved playing in it. I still enjoy a good bluegrass band playing tunes such as "The Orange Blossom Special," "The Wabash Cannonball," and "The Wreck of the Old 97."

Our church was also a social outlet for us young people. Periodically there would be special meetings, when evangelistic speakers would come in from other areas, and they would preach a series of sermons encouraging people to come to faith in Christ. These "revivals" were usually held once a year, every night for about two weeks. They were always a social highlight for me, because for all those evenings in a row I got to be with my buddies and my cousins.

During those meetings, each evening an "invitation" would be given to anyone who wanted to dedicate their life to follow Christ and His teaching. When I was twelve I had a feeling that I should respond. I waited until the last night of the meetings and the last part of the invitation (I guess I was hesitant to take this big step), and then I stood up to be acknowledged as a Christian. It was a decision that would shape the rest of my life, as you will see throughout my story.

One of the things the church taught us was to learn to appreciate the Bible, as God's guidebook for living. When I was 15, I decided I would try to read through the book of Psalms and one verse in particular got my attention. Here is what Psalm 37:4 says:

Delight yourself in the Lord
And He will give you the desires of your heart.

I thought, "Boy, now that's a great promise! When the Maker of the Universe promises to give me the desires of my heart, I'm going to take Him up on it!"

I knew that I had a lot of desires in my heart (like getting away from the isolation of cleaning eggs and feeding chickens), and I took the Lord at His word and believed that He would give those to me, if I

Mim, age 11

would "delight myself" in Him. What exactly did that mean? I wasn't sure, but I made an agreement with Him, that I would learn to delight myself in Him. I had faith that He would give me my heart's desires.

I didn't know it at the time, but one of the eventual "desires of my heart" lived on a nearby farm. There a young girl was growing up who would be my life's partner.

"Mim" (Miriam Esther Hershey), who is now my wife of 64 years, was born on November 29, 1926, to Isaac Hershey, Jr., and Esther Burkhart Hershey in Paradise, Pennsylvania. Just like me, she was raised on a farm, in a Mennonite family in Lancaster County, as the second oldest in her family. She was even named for her mother, just like me.

Her family was all girls for many years. Her parents had three daughters and then twins—also daughters. In a farm family you are looking for boys to help with the work, but those five girls learned how to work hard. They milked cows, fed chickens, harvested potatoes, hoed corn, and picked the worms off of tobacco leaves. Eventually Mim's parents had twin sons and then a third son, making a total of eight children.

Mim's family's farm in Paradise, Pennsylvania, had 70 or 80 acres, big enough to make a living for their large family. The property didn't have a stream, so each day at noon the children helped bring in all the cows so they could drink water. Both of us learned early in our lives that as a farm family you had to "pull together" and do what needed to be done, regardless of whether you felt like doing it.

We also learned that you get a sense of satisfaction when you can see tangible results from your hard work. Many of the farms in Lancaster County are known even today for their neatness, because people take pride in caring for their property. Maybe we found it tedious to weed the corn, or mow the hay, or paint the fence, but at the end of the day we saw the results of our efforts. We knew we had accomplished something.

There wasn't a lot of recreation in Mim's family life, but sometimes in the evening their Dad would play a little softball with them; or in the winter, if they had time, they would go sledding. Her father was a strict disciplinarian; he regularly drilled the children on their multiplication tables and memory work, often at the dinner table. They were expected to do their best in school. He was also fond of music and he made sure each of his eight children learned to play the piano. Some evenings the family would gather around the piano and sing as he played hymns. They attended the Paradise Mennonite Church every week; like my family, her family was very committed to their faith.

Mim became a Christian when she was 15 and she remembers that the catalyst was a bicycle accident. She was riding her bicycle (actually she shared it with her sister) along Route 30 (busy even at that time) after a snow storm. She couldn't see where the cement stopped and the gravel shoulder started, and when the wheels hit the gravel, they slipped out from under her. She was thrown from the bike into a lane of traffic, her school books flying all over the place. Fortunately the traffic on the road could swerve around her, but after that close call she thought she should get more serious about her relationship with God. Like me, she made a public commitment to Christ in her church and her Christian faith was nurtured there.

It's ironic that Mim sold potato chips before I did—and those of a future competitor! At that time farmers would travel to a "farmer's market" in a larger city to sell their produce, supplemented by other items they made or bought for re-sale. In her early teens Mim often spent Saturdays in Philadelphia, leaving before dawn to get there in time to work at a stand that sold things like starter plants for people's gardens, fresh vegetables, pretzels, and potato chips. The chips, which came from Utz, in Hanover, Pennsylvania, were sold at the farmer's market by the ounce. Mim scooped the chips from a large container and placed them in waxed bags for the customers. I'm sure she never dreamed that one day she'd be scooping Herr's potato chips into bags!

At the age of 15, while a sophomore and an excellent student, Mim decided to stop attending high school. The reason may seem odd to you, but I think it's interesting how our life choices affect the future in ways we can't anticipate. At that time it was her perception that when she became a Christian (as I've described above) she would need to start dressing like a Mennonite. She had observed that those in her school who dressed this way were not popular, and she didn't want to face her peers, now that she was going to start dressing "plain." So she just told them she wouldn't be back.

She went home and told her father that she wanted to quit school. Apparently he didn't object and took her to the local magistrate's office to sign the papers for her to quit school early. The official said,

"OK, I assume it's because you need her on the farm."

"No," her father replied honestly. "I don't need her on the farm. She just wants to quit."

"Well, you could just sign the paper anyway, because we need a reason on record."

But her father insisted that he wouldn't sign any such paper because it wasn't true—he didn't need her on the farm.

Mim was appalled. Sitting on the edge of the imposing arm chair nearby, she begged him, "Dad, you *have* to sign those papers. I *can't* go back. I told all the girls I wouldn't be back." But her father was not going to lie.

The magistrate must have seen how desperate she was, so he suggested, "Is there something else that we could give for a reason, like do you want to go to a different school or something? What are you good at?"

Mim had always had an idea that she wanted to be a secretary. She told the magistrate that she was good at numbers (remember all those multiplication drills at the Hershey dinner table) and she thought she would like to learn to type.

The magistrate suggested that she could go to a business school and she jumped at the chance. At least no one there would know her or care that she was dressing "plain." Plus she really was an excellent student and the idea of more schooling appealed to her.

So it was that she set out to enroll in Lancaster Business College. She tells it this way: "I remember it was a Friday night that my dad called the school. Dad was told that the school usually didn't accept students without a high school diploma, but he assured them that I was a very good student. Well, they said, if I came to the school the next Monday, someone would be available to talk to me and maybe they would give it a try. Dad had other obligations that Monday, but he gave me a quarter for the round-trip bus fare to the school on North Queen Street in Lancaster.

"What an unnerving day! I used the quarter to ride the bus into the city and somehow found the school. There a bookkeeping teacher met me and said I could sit in on his class; he said it would cost 25 cents for the textbook. Embarrassed that I had already used my quarter and had no more money, I must have looked pretty unsettled. Kindly, he told me if it was inconvenient I could bring the payment in the next day.

"Sitting there in my homemade cotton dress (I can still visualize the corduroys and jackets of the other students), aware that everyone else was older and had graduated from high school, I still somehow tuned in when the teacher gave the class an oral math question. I computed the answer in my head while the other students were working it out on paper, and I waited for one of them to give the answer. No hands went up. Hmmm, maybe I was wrong. Computing it again, I felt sure it was the correct answer. Timidly I raised my hand and the teacher seemed surprised when I gave the correct answer.

" 'Miss Hershey, how did you arrive at the answer so quickly?' he asked.

" 'I used algebra.' (It was the math course I had been taking as a sophomore in high school.)

"The other students looked at me quizzically. Sure, they had taken algebra in high school, but this was several years later and this was bookkeeping. I'm sure they wondered where this little plain Mennonite girl came from who had wandered into their classroom. I never made many friends there (they were all older and much more sophisticated), but I felt like I could hold my own when it came to the school work, and the teachers must have agreed, because they let me stay, even without my high school diploma.

"After that first day of school, I couldn't remember where the bus stop was and stood on the wrong corner for what seemed like hours. Eventually I saw a lady who looked approachable and I asked her where the bus stop was. She smiled sympathetically and said 'I'll just walk you there,' probably realizing I'd never make it otherwise. My mother was nearly frantic by the time I made it home. But the mission was accomplished, and I was enrolled in a 15-month secretarial course. There I learned typing, bookkeeping, shorthand, and became qualified to work as a legal secretary."

As I look back on Mim's unusual decision to go to business school, I can't help but think the Lord was preparing her already for the future life we would lead together in our business. Typing invoices, keeping track of accounts, organizing the ledgers, filling out tax forms—who would have done all that if it hadn't been for her? She is a meticulous bookkeeper of our personal finances to this day and I know better than to question whether she has paid a bill on time. She also has her father's dogged determination to do everything by the book, not to fudge for convenience or to use the ends to justify the means. I think God honors that integrity.

I actually met Mim by dating her older sister. I had a couple of dates with Evelyn before I found out that I was a "test." She'd had a steady boyfriend before we met and they had decided to date other people before committing to an engagement. After she dated me a few times, she realized that I wasn't the one she wanted!

It could have been pretty devastating to me, except that during one of those dates, I saw Mim at a church function and realized I didn't have *my* first choice either. Mim must have thought I looked OK, too, so we were both glad it worked out that way.

Neither of us had dated many people before we met each other—I was only 19 and she was 17. Dates at that time were often double dates to church events; afterwards we'd go to friends' homes to have a snack and maybe play Rook (a card game popular in our circles at that time) or some other game. Sometimes we went to a sports event or a local fair or farm show, but not often.

During this time I was still working on my father's farm and Mim was going to business college. Later, she began working for a friend of her father, an attorney in Lancaster named Samuel Wenger.

My father had always said we could stop working on the farm when we were 21, so as soon as I celebrated my 21st birthday, I decided I would talk to him. I told my dad that poultry farming was too lonely for me —I didn't have anyone to talk with during the day. I wanted to try another profession. He was fine with my decision, but he said he didn't have any money to help me get started.

So the first thing that started me on my entrepreneurial journey was that I knew I wanted to do something that would get me off the farm so that I could interact more with people. And I had that promise from Psalm 37:4. But without any money or education, what would it be?

∽o∾

Continue to reverence the Lord all the time,
for surely you have a wonderful future ahead of you.
There is hope for you yet!
Proverbs 23:17, 18

Business Principles

If you are in a profession you don't enjoy, be willing to make a change. I've known people who resign themselves to a job they detest and then complain about it their whole lives.

Learn to enjoy the satisfaction that comes from working hard and seeing tangible results.

∽◦∾

The lazy man is full of excuses. "I can't go to work!" he says.
"If I go outside I might meet a lion in the street and be killed!"
Proverbs 22:13

Jim, age 21

Chapter 2

AN OPPORTUNITY FOR CHANGE

E very day I would sit and clean eggs, eggs, and more eggs. And every day I would eagerly search the newspaper for leads on a different kind of job. I started looking in August (right after my birthday) and I believe it was March of the next year before I saw anything that I thought would be remotely feasible.

I saw that a potato chip business was for sale in Lancaster that cost $1,750.00. Now, I didn't have any attraction to potato chips, because snacking was not common in our home—we were too frugal for that. But it struck me that here was a business that seemed doable and affordable.

∽o∾

The intelligent man is always open to new ideas.
In fact, he looks for them.
Proverbs 18:15

∽o∾

Not that I had the money, or knew anything about going to a bank and getting a loan. My Dad always took care of the finances for our family and I didn't know that getting a bank loan was an option.

If I were looking to start a business today, I might make use of a resource like the Small Business Administration, which was founded by an act of Congress in 1953 to "aid, counsel, assist and protect, insofar as is possible, the interests of small business concerns." Over the years, Herr's has looked to the SBA for loans and help with growing our company. I would encourage you, if you are interested in starting a business, to go to their website, *www.SBA.gov*, for help.

But if the SBA had existed in 1946, I probably wouldn't have known about it. As I was thinking of how I could get the cash I needed, a possibility came to mind—maybe I could ask Mim's boss to loan me the money. I knew that he was a successful attorney and I thought he might be willing to give me a chance to get started.

Without further ado (and without mentioning it to Mim), I told the owners I thought I'd be interested and took them to Mr. Wenger's office to see if he would give me a loan.

Mim tells about that day in 1946, when I went to ask for the loan, like this: "I was in my side office of the law firm, where I could see

Mim, age 19

the main area of the office, and I saw a young man come into the room with a buxom peroxide blonde. To my surprise, Jim was with them! The three of them said they wanted to see Mr. Wenger. Jim waltzed right by me with the couple and entered Mr. Wenger's office. Mr. Wenger came out of his office some minutes later and told me to write out a note for $1,750 to Mr. Herr. I was thinking, 'What on earth is Jim doing with that couple and why does he need money?' Jim came by my desk and said, 'I'll call you tonight.' I was thinking, 'You bet you will.' "

When I saw Mim that night I told her of my plan to purchase Verna's Potato Chips, located on Charlotte Street in Lancaster. For my investment of $1,750, I would receive two iron kettles, each capable of holding one hundred pounds of lard, a three-potato slicer, a peeler that held ten pounds of potatoes, and a 1936 Dodge panel truck in fair condition. The deal also included a part-time employee and a rented building.

Iron kettle used in the Lancaster location and tobacco shed

Mim knew how much I wanted to get a job where I could be around people instead of sitting by myself and cleaning eggs. Still, when I first told her of my plans, she thought the idea was way off the wall. What did we know about making potato chips? All I knew was, I had to repay that loan, or I'd not only lose the business but I'd lose my girlfriend as well.

The former owners, neither of whom was "Verna," promised to stay on the job for two weeks to teach me the business. Two days after the sale was completed, however, they abruptly departed and I never saw them again.

After being in the chip business for about three months, I wasn't sure if I had made the right decision in selecting my new profession.

our Wedding day

The morning of our wedding day was cloudy with just a little rain. About 10:00 it cleared off into a beautiful day. Shortly after 7:30 the cooks, consisting mostly of neighbors, arrived and soon there was the wonderful sound of friendly hurrying about setting tables, preparing food, arranging flowers, etc.

Finally 11:00 came, the hour we had so happily awaited. The trio began singing and -- we were married. Truly, it was the happiest moment of our life. After the delicious dinner we went to Lancaster to have our pictures taken while the second tables of guests were being served. Then there was the happy afternoon, filled with handshakes and best wishes from loved ones, admiring the beautiful gifts, and laughingly posing for snapshots. How wonderful it is to know that God has pronounced us husband and wife and that we will go thru life together.

About 4 o'clock amid farewells, and a due amount of confetti, crepe paper and tin cans, we left for our 2 wks. honeymoon. It was a perfect day.

Mim's diary description of their wedding day

people—which necessitated two seatings in the Hershey home. Two weeks later my parents had a similar dinner in our home for more of our relatives. Both of us are from large extended families.

At that time the Mennonite church did not approve of wearing jewelry, so we didn't give each other wedding bands. My gift to Mim? A very practical sewing machine! She still has it and it still works.

When we set off on our honeymoon, we had $250.00 and a two-door red Dodge that I was very proud of—the first car I bought that was not used. We thought we wanted to go to Florida so we headed south, but that's the closest we came to having travel plans. We had no reservations anywhere and neither of us had ever stayed in a motel before. I remember our first stop was a little cabin near Baltimore that had linoleum on the floors.

We made it to Florida, and one day we stopped at a touristy reptile farm. The establishment also had a game of chance, a big spinning wheel where patrons paid for a number and the wheel was spun to determine if your number was a winner. Well, we tried the wheel and we didn't win. The man at the wheel said we should try again and we'd surely win. We tried and of course lost again. We spent more money than we should have—I think we lost $30. This unsuccessful gambling venture caused us to be short of money for the rest of our trip. We went home by way of Sterling, Illinois, where I had relatives I thought we could stay with. I borrowed $25 from them so we could return to our home in Willow Street.

Wedding Gift

The "honeymoon suite"!
A little cabin near Baltimore

The red Dodge on the beach, Daytona, FL – on Jim and Mim's honeymoon

∽o∽

Wealth from gambling quickly disappears;
wealth from hard work grows.

Proverbs 13:11

∽o∽

Though the reptile farm story is not something I'm proud of, and I certainly do not espouse gambling, I do think it makes a point that I have a certain tolerance for taking risks. I don't know if that's something you're born with, but most entrepreneurs I know have had to be willing to take a risk of some kind—hopefully with much more common sense than I had at the reptile farm!—in order to get a business started. My loan from Mr. Wenger was of course the greater risk, because it involved our livelihood.

As I look back, I think you have to have a certain optimism that you can accomplish what you set out to do—maybe more so than sometimes seems realistic to most people. Of greatest value to me was that I have a supportive life partner. Mim has always been like a trooper about hanging in there with me, through good risks and bad—and I'll tell you about some of those later in the book.

Business Principles

If you want to create a business you have to be on the lookout for an opportunity. It doesn't usually just come to you—you have to be willing to make the effort to look for it.

Be willing to ask for help. Think about the people you know—is there anyone who could give you that leg up you need? If someone knows you are looking for a start, they may be willing to give you a hand.

Don't let a lack of resources keep you from your dream. Explore all the options available to you.

∽ο∽

The diligent man makes good use of everything he finds.
Proverbs 12:27b

In 2011 Jim and Mim stand beside a replica of a 1936 Dodge panel truck, like the one he purchased with Verna's Potato Chips in 1946.

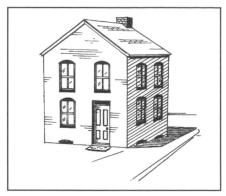

*Sketch of Herr's first location.
"Verna's" in Lancaster (Charlotte Street) 1946*

Tobacco Shed on Herr Farm 1947

West Willow Bakery 1949

Chapter 3

EARLY DAYS OF HERR'S

The final years of World War II were not an optimal time to begin a food company. Gas had been rationed, along with sugar and other commodities during the war. However, both Mim and I had learned from growing up in the Depression that it is possible to survive in hard times. Neither of us was afraid of hard work, and we were committed to the farm-family philosophy of "pulling together" to make something work. So with our newly-wed optimism we set to work.

∽⚭∾

Hard work brings prosperity;
playing around brings poverty.
Proverbs 28:19

∽⚭∾

Shortly after I purchased the business I changed the name to Herr's Potato Chips. I didn't want someone else's name on the bag, especially Verna's—I didn't even know who she was!

I would begin my day by peeling, slicing, and cooking the potato chips. I had one employee, Mrs. Armstrong (I don't remember her first name), who helped me half a day. During the afternoon, we would pack the chips into pound-size cans, half-pound cans, and five-cent bags. Before we were married, when Mim was still working for Mr. Wenger, I'd pick her up after her workday at the law firm and together we would finish packaging the chips, put them in the panel truck, and drive through Lancaster to sell them door-to-door. I went to Cabbage Hill and then down on Duke and Lime streets. Early on, we were bringing in $36.00 a week in sales.

Later I decided to move the business from Charlotte Street in Lancaster to the town of Willow Street, where my family's farm was located (by that time it was owned by my older brother). There was a vacant tobacco shed on the property that I thought would be the right size for making the potato chips. My brother agreed to rent it to me for our operation.

After we got married Mim worked full time with me and we rented an "apartment" in the Herr family farmhouse for $25.00 a month. We had three large rooms—one upstairs and two downstairs. The accommodations were sparse and didn't include indoor plumbing, but it was just down the lane from the tobacco shed, so we had no commute!

We worked long hours, often beginning the work day at 4:00 A.M. and not finishing until 11:00 P.M. We had learned from growing up on farms that long days are often necessary when there is work to be done. You don't think about it or question it—you just do what needs to be done. In our case, we needed to have the chips made and ready to sell by the afternoon, and in the evening we needed to have the potatoes and oil ready to make chips again the next morning.

Herr Family Farmhouse
Jim and Mim lived in several rooms in the back in their early marriage.

Sometimes in the evening we would drive 40 miles west to Hanover, Pennsylvania, to take chips to a distributor who was paying us 35 cents for a dozen five-cent bags. He would then take the chips to New York and sell them for 45 or 50 cents; he didn't make much money and the venture did not last.

Other evenings we would have to drive an hour or so south to the Baltimore Harbor to purchase potatoes for the next day. I usually bought potatoes from a local grower, but when local potatoes weren't available, we needed the ones from Florida that were shipped to Baltimore. It was often because of these trips that we were up late at night, trying to get ready for the next morning's work. Mim also did all the bookwork in the evenings.

Eventually I got tired of selling chips to individuals door-to-door. It was a hassle to find people at home, especially the customers who owed me money! I remember one lady in particular, who was never "available" to pay me, yet she always had her radio blaring and the lights on—I knew she was inside. At one point she owed me $5.00. I decided I didn't want to spend my time collecting money, so I looked into what it would take to sell to stores instead of individuals.

I didn't have a clue what to charge the stores, but I did some research on what competitors were charging and just went with that. I don't remember the first store that became a customer, but early on I sold some chips to a drugstore. The day before Christmas the gentleman who ran the drugstore asked me if I wanted a drink to celebrate the season. I thought he meant a Coke, so I said OK. He gave me some whiskey and it burned all the way down my throat. Then he offered me a chaser, but I didn't know what that was so I said, "No, I think I'll leave well enough alone!"

I loved selling (here was my chance to talk to people) and gradually I added additional stores to the route and our business expanded. Though we had stiff competition from other potato chip companies operating in the Lancaster area, we were growing too.

After two years on my brother's farm, I realized we were outgrowing our space. I looked around for a facility and found a 3,600-square-foot bakery located nearby in West Willow. The owners had stopped baking bread and the building was vacant. We rented the bakery as well as an adjacent house for our residence.

I called the landlord shortly after we moved there to ask if we could take in another boarder. He reminded me that the lease only allowed two. Then I announced that we had a new baby girl, and of course he was delighted. Miriam June (we call her June) was born in 1949, and two years later our son James Melvin, now known as J.M., was born.

We had added several full-time employees before moving to the bakery. The first employees hired at the farm were relatives and neighbors. We didn't advertise in newspapers or formally interview people. We just gave people a chance and if someone wasn't working as expected, we encouraged them to find another job.

When we needed additional help, we usually looked to our circle of friends. Dave Huber, a schoolmate of mine who had grown up on the farm next to ours, opened a public accounting service in Willow Street. When we were located at the bakery in West Willow, I hired his company to do our accounting, and he personally kept our books for nearly twenty years, even after we moved out of the area.

I hired my best friend, Harold Groff, along with Charlie Myers, to work in sales. As the business with stores increased, we hired two more salesmen: One was a salesman for a milk company, Art Herman, and the other was another good friend, Ben Fenninger.

I actually met Ben when I was dating Mim, because he was living in an apartment on Mim's dad's farm and working part time on the farm. He was also working for Armstrong Industries in Lancaster. When I was looking for additional sales people, I thought of Ben and offered him a job at a salary of $65 a week, but he told me he couldn't leave Armstrong for that money. Later, he developed a skin rash from the working conditions at Armstrong (he was allergic to something in the plant) and when I asked him another time if he

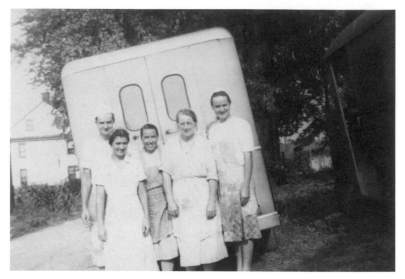

Left to Right: Jim, Mim, Employee Mary Pickel, Jim's Mother, Jim's sister Mary, 1947

wanted to work in sales for us, he accepted. I think we increased the offer by $5 or $10 a week.

Ben is a "people person" and I knew he would be a good salesman. I remember early in his employment we were working together on a sales route in Coatesville. The early trucks didn't have passenger seats so I sat on a potato chip can. The truck had a manual transmission and Ben wasn't used to shifting gears. We were stopped at a red light and when the light turned green he put the truck in gear and took off—and so did I! I flew off the potato chip can into the back of the truck. Ben was sure that would be his last day on the job, but he was a loyal employee for many years.

The truck Ben was driving was one of the pair of step-vans I purchased new in 1949. One was a Studebaker and the other was a Chevrolet. We needed the trucks to cover routes that expanded from Lancaster to include West Chester and Coatesville, as well as Wilmington, Delaware.

Ben became the first salesman to be paid on commission. His route was returning less than $700 in sales and we paid him a flat ten percent commission on sales. When I told him I wanted the routes to return $1,000 a week, Ben didn't tell me he thought I was crazy but I knew he thought it. When he was the first salesman to hit $1,000 on a route, I reminded him, "I told you that you would." Ben eventually became our first sales manager and Art Herman served as our first credit manager.

In those early years we terminated very few people. We fired one person for being dishonest (a customer reported him). Another salesman was dishonest but we didn't know about the theft at first. One day the man told his wife that after he was dead she was to tell us that he owed us money. She told him to go and tell us immediately. He sweated it out but he did it.

About this time I decided that cooking the potato chips was not the best use of my time, so I hired Lewis Gehman to take over the task. Lew had learned many of his skills by cooking doughnuts for soldiers in the United States Army. He had the foresight to see ways in which we could operate more efficiently, and he was good at fixing problems. When he took over the cooking, I went on the road to sell and build routes. After the routes were developed, I would turn them over to salesmen to maintain.

Jim & Mim responded affirmatively to an invitation to "help with the work" at a new mission church near Oxford. (The mission was started by the church they attended, Willow Street Mennonite Church.)

Lew became our production manager and worked faithfully with me until his retirement in 1984. With help from some of our suppliers, I learned about new and better cooking processes. We constructed a new kettle measuring three feet by five feet and had burners installed. At first we used lard in the kettle, but we switched to corn oil due to our customers' preferences. That was a big decision, as Herr's became known as a "lighter" chip. Today we offer a product called "Old Fashioned," a lard-cooked chip that is manufactured for us, but throughout most of our history our products have been fried in vegetable oil.

As I learned the business, I began to enjoy having my own company, and as I began to network with others in the industry I started to appreciate the snack food business. Two years after I had borrowed the money from Mr. Wenger I paid back my loan, and I was glad I had stuck it out.

It helped that because of what Mim had learned at Lancaster Business College she could take care of the accounting. As we worked together, God was working things out for us, just as He promised in Psalm 37:4.

As I saw the Lord's goodness in keeping His promise to give me the desires of my heart, I also began to learn what the verse means about "delighting yourself in Him." Mim and I were asked to help teach at a small mission church, located near Oxford, Pennsylvania. It was a 25-mile drive from our home in West Willow, and, though it was a stretch to drive that far several times a week, helping to get that little church started was one way we could delight ourselves in serving Him.

Business Principles

Be willing to work hard to make something "go." Don't think
so much about how long the hours are or that others are not
working as hard as you are. Be committed to your own goal and
stick to it.

If you are married, be sure you "pull together" at your work.
Even if your spouse is not working in the business, it takes
commitment from both of you, because there are going to be
times when you get too discouraged or tired to keep going if
you don't have that support from each other.

Don't give up too quickly. At first I thought I had made a wrong
decision about making potato chips, but as I stuck with it I
learned to appreciate the business.

Chapter 4

FIRE!

The afternoon of September 5, 1951, I was selling chips in Wilmington, Delaware, and my time was getting away from me. I knew we had some folks coming to the house that evening for a prayer meeting and it was already 5:30. I called Mim and told her I'd be late—to go ahead and eat and give the kids their evening baths without me, because I'd barely make it home in time for the meeting.

As Mim was giving June her bath on the second floor of our home, she glanced out the window and spotted flames coming from the potato chip plant (we still called it the bakery). The workday had concluded, the employees had left for the day, and none of the equipment was operating. Cooking oil had dripped onto a hot fire brick and burst into flames.

Within minutes the building was fully engulfed in fire. Our home and the bakery building were separated by only twelve feet.

"I was looking outside towards the old bake shop," Mim recalls. "I can still see those flames licking the white-framed building. I scooped up June, wrapped her in a towel, and called the local fire company. By that time, the fire was roaring and the old frame building was pretty

Mim with J.M. and June

much gone. J.M., our six-month-old baby, was asleep in a carriage and I took June and him outside. Figuring our house would burn along with the bakery, I made sure I had a pacifier and went to the neighbor's, our landlord Ted Bowers. I sat on the bank in their yard with my children and just watched the bakery burn."

Mim recalls passersby stopping to offer aid as the fire trucks arrived. A couple of sailors were on their way to the Bainbridge Naval Training Center, and they went into the house and carried out the furniture. We had only furnished a few rooms, so there wasn't much, except for a "treasure" we had—our baby grand piano, which was a gift from Mim's father (he made sure each of his married children had a piano in their home). The sailors quickly carried it outside and put it in a nearby field.

I was oblivious to it all, just trying to make it home in time for the prayer meeting. When I got closer to our place, I began to see fire trucks and bedlam. There were lots of cars along the road, and they seemed to be in front of where we lived. Imagine my panic when I realized that it was my family and my business that were in jeopardy! When I saw Mim and the kids on our neighbor's lawn, I was so relieved they were safe.

I immediately knew that the building was a total loss. It was a combustible building and it had been leveled in a hurry. The fire was so hot that we could see blistered paint on the bathroom door where Mim had been bathing June, but no other damage had taken place to the house, because some of the firemen had gone to the roof and sprayed it with water to keep the fire from destroying it.

All four of our parents arrived at the scene to help us. Mim's father secured hamburgers for the firemen. The furniture was carried back into the home, but when we went to take the piano back in, there was no way it would fit through the door without taking the legs off. We still don't know how those sailors got the piano out. Mim and I stayed in our home that night but the children stayed with my parents until we could re-group.

What a confusing time that was! We had been engrossed in making and selling potato chips and then all of a sudden, there was a 180-degree shift—everything was gone!

Salesman Ben Fenninger had loaded his truck the afternoon before. The day following the fire, when he was delivering Herr's chips in Coatesville, a delivery milkman saw him and asked, "What are you doing here?" Ben didn't know what he meant, and the guy told him the plant had burned. Ben said, "No, it didn't." The milkman then pulled out a copy of a newspaper with a story on the fire. He called me right away and I had to admit that in my confusion I hadn't even let him know what had happened.

❧

We can make our plans,
but the final outcome is in God's hands.
Proverbs 16:1

❧

The insurance man came to our home the next day and offered us $4,000 for the loss of the business. This was taking into account that our trucks did not burn because they were on the road, and our car was fine.

Mim and I discussed whether we should rebuild or do something different. We had to make a quick decision, because if we were not going to continue the business, we would have to tell our customers (not to mention our employees) that the business was closing. If we were going to continue, we'd have to somehow get chips to our customers until we could rebuild.

It was a decision that would influence the rest of our lives, but it didn't take us long to make. We would keep going. I'm not sure what other options we had, except I thought I could possibly work on my brother's farm. But by now we had five years of experience in business, a base of customers, and employees we enjoyed working with. I also had learned to know some people in the industry who I felt might help us.

One of those was Si Musser, owner of Charles Chips, and he graciously responded to our need. Si knew that if they were in trouble we would help them. I also knew the Utz family; both companies agreed to sell us bulk chips in big cans, from which we scooped out chips to fill our bags. It was the best we could do. We had to take care of our customers.

We were so grateful to my father for offering us the use of his two-car garage in Willow Street as a base to pack the chips to keep the business operating, but of course that was a short-term solution. We began searching for another location to manufacture Herr's chips.

The search included the area around Oxford, Pennsylvania. We were traveling in that direction because of our work at Mount Vernon Mennonite Church. Mim and I felt a lot of loyalty to that little church, and to be located closer would mean we could be of greater help there. We knew it would mean it would be less convenient to visit our parents and siblings, but we both had the desire to give our extra time to the church. We learned that there was a plot of 13 acres available in the town of Oxford, so we seriously considered buying that for our new location.

Now it happened that John and Miriam Thomas, another young couple who were helping with the mission church at Mount Vernon, learned of a house with some property in Nottingham (just three miles from Oxford) that they brought to our attention. Through the years our paths have crossed with the Thomases' many times (John and most of their children have worked at Herr's, we worked on many church projects together, and their youngest son is married to our youngest daughter), but perhaps the most far-reaching comment John ever made to me was to recommend that we take a look at this house.

We learned that the property on which the house was located included 45 acres and not only the house but also an old barn. We were impressed with the property and we liked the house, but the asking price was $20,000, an amount we just couldn't come up with.

We believed the Lord would lead us to the right spot, so we prayed and somehow felt the Nottingham land was the way we should go. Eventually the owners agreed to sell us 37 acres for $18,000. We can see now that it's good we didn't buy the site in Oxford, because we didn't realize how much the business would grow and 13 acres wouldn't have accommodated our growth.

～○～

In everything you do, put God first, and he will direct
you and crown your efforts with success.
Proverbs 3:6

～○～

The property we purchased is the current site of our Nottingham plant. Later, we purchased an additional 13 acres, the location of our corporate offices. Throughout our 65 years we have acquired additional acreage, much of which we now irrigate with the water we use in processing potatoes.

Financing for the purchase and rebuilding of the plant came from small loans from family members and a loan from a local bank. Both my parents and Mim's parents loaned us $5,000, money that we quickly repaid. Family and friends helped by tearing down the barn on the property and re-using the timber in the new 4,500-square-foot factory we constructed at a cost of $11,000.

My uncle Clarence Herr, who was helping in the rebuilding, suggested the new plant should be constructed in the middle of the property. We didn't take his advice, but years later, when we needed additional space, the plant was moved to the center of the property—exactly where he said it should go in the first place!

Money was scarce, but we believed we made a good purchase. Someone from Rising Sun, Maryland, later offered us $20,000 for the house alone. I'm glad we didn't take the offer. We kept the home, renting out the top floor and living on the first floor. We paid the $80.00-a-month mortgage with the rent. This is the house we live in today (both floors!).

Business Principles

Sometimes the unforeseen happens, and you just can't make it without the help of others. Don't be too proud to ask for help. We could never have made it through this period if we had tried to do everything on our own. Be willing to acknowledge the help of others and the help of the Lord to get you through the tough times. A business requires more than any one person or family can offer.

When people offer you advice, listen carefully but then make your own decisions. We made some that were right and some that weren't, but in the end you have to make the decision and accept the responsibility for it.

∾o∾

The wise man is glad to be instructed,
but a self-sufficient fool falls flat on his face.
Proverbs 10:8

The house on the 37-acre Nottingham property, 1952

Chapter 5

REBUILDING AND GROWTH IN NOTTINGHAM

While the cost of rebuilding was covered by loans, I had no money for working capital to begin production. I tried my local banker but money was tight and he decided their bank had loaned me as much as they were willing. I had already asked my family and friends for so much help, I didn't want to ask for more. I didn't know where to turn.

One of the construction workers building the plant mentioned to me that he personally knew a banker in Newark, Delaware, and he thought he might be willing to loan me some money. Leaving no stone unturned, I headed to Newark. Sure enough, after listening to my impassioned plea for help, Mr. Matthews issued me a bank loan for $1,500.00. That boosted my spirits enough that I decided to make one more purchase before we began our Nottingham operation.

∽∾

You are a poor specimen if you can't stand
the pressure of adversity.
Proverbs 24:10

I had not used the insurance money for the construction of the plant because I had felt it was important to start in our new facility with a different type of cooker to allow us greater production capacity. I learned that there was a used automatic cooker for sale in Boston that could process 100 pounds of chips an hour (the old iron kettle we had used in the West Willow bakery could process a maximum of 40 pounds an hour). I knew this could make a huge difference to our company. So after I had gotten the vote of confidence from the Newark banker, I headed to Boston to purchase the new cooker.

By the spring of 1952—just six months after the fire—we were back in operation. Several of our key employees from West Willow decided to stay with our company and drive the distance to Nottingham each day. I feel it was their loyalty and hard work that were vital to our company's ability to transition to a new level of growth. My parents drove to Nottingham every day to help us, and picked up Mary Mowrer, an early employee, on the way.

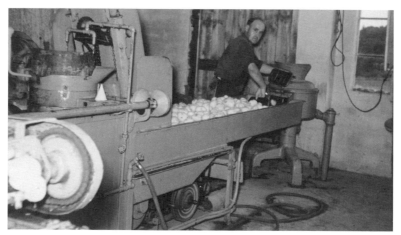

Jim's father operating the potato peeler, spring 1952

Nottingham—how we have grown to love this town! The first Christmas we were here, I took a can of chips and a Christmas greeting to each of our neighbors; it was the beginning of many decades of good relationships with them. In fact, recently we went to the funeral of the last of our generation to live in our section of Nottingham, a poignant reminder of how time moves along!

One young teenager I met that first Christmas, John Featherman, lived with his parents just two doors away from us, and as we talked he agreed to work for the company at odd jobs if we had a special need. For example, one day we asked him to go to Baltimore and purchase salt, because we were nearly out—that kind of thing. Over the course of time, we developed a special friendship with this young man, keeping up with him as he went off to Penn State, then the United States Navy, then law school. John went on to become a very successful Chester County attorney, often representing Herr's in legal matters.

As the business grew, we were always interested in buying neighboring properties, and often John would handle the legal work for us. Early on we were involved in a transaction where the seller grew quite unreasonable and John was frustrated about it. I remember telling John that it was okay, that if both parties don't feel like they're being treated fairly, the deal shouldn't take place anyway. If you take advantage of someone, I reminded him, your reputation will be tarnished and you won't be able to make the next deal. He later told me that he learned a lesson that day in treating others with respect (even if they are contentious).

Trucks at loading dock, 1956

I treasure our relationship with people like John—we have a history together. I like to do business locally as much as I can, giving support to the community from which we draw so much benefit. Those early years were years of rapid expansion, and Nottingham was the epicenter.

It wasn't just Herr's that was expanding, though—the whole snack food industry exploded in the 1950s. It was the post-War boom and people were moving from rural to urban settings, from farming to manufacturing. More leisure time was available and television was introduced into people's homes. Americans began to look forward to snacking while they watched their favorite TV shows, and as the customer base increased so did advertising on television. Some of the major companies began to advertise salty snacks on TV, and it helped increase consumer awareness for the whole industry.

We advertised on the radio that our chips were "lively, light, and delicious," and they really were. Our market share grew, especially with Acme markets in the 1960s and 1970s in the Philadelphia region. Our salesmen used to say that they could open a bag of chips, and the chips would sell themselves.

But it was not a time for resting on our laurels. As the snack food industry grew, we needed to keep abreast of it all. I think it's important to keep informed about what others are doing in your line of work, to see what you can learn in order to give yourself a leg up. We didn't innovate just to be the first to do something, but we were pretty quick to take advantage of new ways of doing things. I found that using up-to-date equipment soon paid for itself.

Packaging equipment was one innovation that we took advantage of. You can lose lots of money if the bags consistently have more than the weight listed on the bag, and of course the law requires that they can't have less. So weights are a big deal in manufacturing, and today, 60 years later, we are using equipment so advanced that the weights of our packages are accurate to the weight of one chip. But in the beginning, someone used to have to scoop the chips into a bag, put the bag on the scale, and then individually adjust the weight of each bag. You can imagine how much time that took, and how getting better equipment could improve that process.

I purchased up-to-date packaging equipment early on. The Woodman Company had developed an Air-Weigh System that consisted of a bin (to hold the freshly cooked chips) in the center of a rotating system of chutes like spokes around the hub of a wheel.

The chutes had doors that allowed just the right weight of chips to fall into a bag at the end of the chute. After the bag was filled with chips, someone had to remove the bag and run it through the heat sealer, then place it in a box on a cart. Once it was full, the cart was then rolled to the nearby dock for the salesmen to pick up.

Meanwhile, the chutes kept turning, and someone had to be ready on the other side to put bags on the chutes for the chips to fall into. You couldn't be dozing off on that job, or there'd be chips all over the floor. Actually, Mim became one of the best operators of that machine. She did that, or she worked on the accounting, while June and J.M. took their naps, each in a seat of our car parked at the loading dock. She was a great multi-tasker! She has always been the most organized person I know.

Mim and Mary Mowrer packing chips

Cans of chips had to be dumped into packaging equipment.

I should also explain how the chips got into the bin to be packed. There was a big can at the end of the cooker, collecting all the newly fried chips, and when it got full a person had to carry it over to the packing equipment, go up some stairs, and dump it into the bin. Now, with all of our conveyer belts and automation, it's hard to remember that people used to have to actually carry the product from one step to the next.

Lew Gehman, our production manager, was busy running the cooker and then filling the packers, and I could soon see that he had to have help. One of our applicants was Harold Blank, a young man just out of high school who had grown up on a nearby farm. I thought about the work ethic required on a farm, and I knew he would understand the mentality that says, "You just do whatever has to be done, and don't worry about a job description." So we hired him to help Lew.

Harold began working at Herr's in 1960 by carrying chips from the cooker to the packer; he then progressed to operating the automatic potato peeler. Later Harold began running the cooker and was named production manager when Lew retired; eventually he was made Senior Vice President of Manufacturing. He was responsible for our many plant expansions and the equipment layout over the years. He retired in 2009, after 49 years of "doing what had to be done."

Harold has been successful at a great diversity of positions for us, just like many of our long-term employees. I like to see people develop and expand their own personal horizons, as well as those of the company. If there is a new position open, rather than always hiring someone new, I like to give the current employees a chance to learn and grow.

One of the people Harold brought on to help with production was another local farm-boy, Dan Jackson. Dan started with Herr's in sales, then became a key long-term production manager at Herr's.

Another key employee in those early years in Nottingham was Charles Temple. He was the kind of engineer who could fix anything. As we grew and got more equipment, we needed him to figure out how to make it all work. He came up with new ideas for conveying the chips from one piece of equipment to another, as well as a monorail system to take packed cases to the warehouse. He also set up the truck garage and maintenance shop. When I think of what people like Lew, Harold, and Charles offered our company, I'm reminded that I hired a lot of people who knew more than I did about their work. You have to rely on the knowledge of others and let them take a project and run with it.

∽०∾

Plans go wrong with too few counselors;
many counselors bring success.
Proverbs 15:22

∽०∾

Our truck routes expanded two or three at a time, and salesmen and additional trucks were added when needed. As I've said, the salesmen supplied the Herr's products directly to the stores through our Direct Store Delivery (DSD) system, a valuable asset of Herr Foods today. This is a relatively expensive method of distributing our products, but it guarantees store managers that every package is fresh. And we've always been blessed with good salesmen through the years.

Mim and I were still very active in the Mount Vernon Mennonite Church, and our pastor's oldest son eventually became a 45-year employee. Jim Kreider was a teenager in the Sunday School class we taught, and when he was a junior in high school I asked him to go with me on a sales call to York, Pennsylvania. I always liked him and thought he'd be a good worker, so when he graduated from high school I hired him to work at the plant. Sure enough, he turned out to be the kind of person who knew how to work hard and was willing to do whatever he was asked.

I think Jim's first job was unloading potatoes. At that time we got potatoes in 100-pound bags and they had to be unloaded from trucks, cut open, and dumped into the potato peeler. It was a tough job, but there was hardly anyone who didn't help with that job from time to time, including Mim! Just like on the farm, we did whatever had to be done whether it was in our "job description" or not! After Jim got married, he and his wife Rozie even came and stayed with our children when Mim and I would go to conventions.

∽∘∼

A faithful employee is as refreshing
as a cool day in the hot summertime.
Proverbs 25:13

∽∘∼

Mim and I started attending snack food industry meetings as early as the late 1940s. Our first national convention was in Ohio, and there were so many chippers there we all decided to form regional meetings. After about five years I was asked to become involved in the governing body and eventually became chairman of the Eastern Region. There I grew to know my competitors and we could talk about common problems and concerns. We discussed potato crops and what was new in the industry. Sometimes, it was kind of funny the game of bluff we played, as we sought each other's advice but didn't want to be too helpful to each other!

But I don't think we have ever had a competitor that we couldn't talk to and be friendly with. Of course, each is interested in growing his own company, so we would fight for sales, but we all understood that and still got along well personally.

Eventually (in 1979) I became president of the national organization, known then as the Potato Chip Institute and now as the Snack Food Association, which opened my eyes to the role that our United States government plays in our business environment. In fact, I think that subject is worth a chapter of its own.

Business Principles

Money is your tool for operation, and sometimes your most pressing job as a businessperson is to find the resources that will allow your business to thrive. Don't give up easily—if you are passionate about what you are doing, you may find someone who will believe in you enough to give you the loan you need to take the next step. Be persistent and try to stay optimistic.

Become connected with people in your industry and learn all you can from them. Try to stay abreast of new ways of doing things and don't be afraid of change.

Be open to giving employees opportunities to diversify in their career paths. If a new position is needed, perhaps someone you already employ would be energized by the challenge of learning something new.

Chapter 6

AN APPRECIATION FOR OUR COUNTRY

❧

Godliness exalts a nation,
but sin is a reproach to any people.
Proverbs 14:34

❧

Most of us don't know what it's like to be restricted from practicing our beliefs or from pursuing our careers. I hope it always stays like that in America.

This wasn't the case for my family in earlier generations. The Herr family migrated from Switzerland to Germany in the seventeenth century because of religious persecution. The Catholic Church called them heretics (for their belief in only adult baptism) and the Protestants called them law-breakers (for their refusal to go to war). But they had a reputation as good farmers and hard workers, so they were invited to go and help rebuild an area of Germany that had been severely damaged by the Thirty Years' War.

Settling in Germany, where the ravages of war had burned the buildings and left the land overgrown with brush, was challenging enough, but soon another war broke out. Faced with more persecution and ever-increasing taxes, in 1710 a group of Mennonites decided to risk the hazardous voyage to America, where they had heard there was land and freedom available.

The way they settled in Pennsylvania was that William Penn, who had converted to the Quaker faith (similar to that of the Mennonites in many ways), experienced religious persecution and he wanted to protect others who suffered for their faith. He granted a settlement in what is now Lancaster County to nine Mennonite men in the early eighteenth century.

The oldest building that is still standing from that early settlement is a house that was built in 1719 by one of my ancestors, Hans Herr, a bishop in the Mennonite church. (That house has been restored to its colonial-era appearance and is now a museum in Lancaster County.) The new settlers used their farming skills and work ethic to develop the area where I grew up; in fact our farm was less than a mile away from the Hans Herr house.

Photo Courtesy of 1719 Hans Herr House and Museum

1719 Hans Herr House

As I was growing up, though, I didn't know anything about Hans Herr or the persecution that had driven my ancestors to Pennsylvania. I knew we Mennonites were different from the general culture, but we didn't suffer any persecution or even prejudice that I can remember. We were enough of a sub-culture that in our day-to-day lives on our farms we were mostly surrounded by people like us.

As I got into business, my perspective began to change. I began to interact with people from other areas of our country and with Christians of other denominations, and I realized that there are other ways to look at things. Over the years I've become more ecumenical and less separatist than some in my denomination.

Though as a young man I didn't even vote, as I became more involved in the snack food industry, I became very interested in politics and in protecting the business environment from government legislation that would hurt someone's chances of starting a small business. I knew that I had been blessed to experience the wonderful freedom we have in this country and I wanted to be sure it would be there for others.

At the time we began the business, we simply hired the people we wanted to hire, we paid them what we could afford to pay them, we bought and sold supplies at the best prices, and we created our own working environment. As I saw more and more legislation being introduced that would restrict business, I wanted to become involved. Sometimes politicians don't realize the adverse effect their well-intentioned laws can have on people's freedom to start small. This has a ripple effect through the economy, because if you discourage small business you take away a lot of jobs those businesses

Jim discusses small business issues with President George Bush during a national leadership conference in Washington, D.C.

could have created. After all, small businesses create the majority of new jobs and employ the most people in our country.

Through my work in the Snack Food Association, I learned of an organization called the National Federation of Independent Business (NFIB). The NFIB is a non-profit, non-partisan organization that was founded in 1943, and it is considered the guardian of, and advocate for, small and independent businesses. The organization educates members on both economic and political issues, and it seeks to guard our free enterprise system.

I became a member of NFIB in 1955, and I've been a member ever since. In 1972 I was asked to become a member of the Board of Directors, and in 1991 I became the chairman, a position I held at the time of the sudden death of our NFIB president, John Sloan. The Board asked me to replace him, and I agreed that I would serve as president and CEO for six months until they could find a replacement. I knew I should stay focused on Herr's, though during this period I learned how capable and responsible our employees were; they kept the business strong in my frequent absences.

During those six months that I was NFIB's president, in January, 1992, it happened that President George H. W. Bush decided to take a group of U.S. businessmen to the Far East on a 12-day trade mission. One of the people on their invitation list was the president of NFIB, so there I was! I happened to be at the right spot at the right time. It was one of the greatest honors I've experienced—to ride in Air Force One and to interact with people like the presidents of

Business leaders accompany Bush

These business leaders will be with President Bush at various times during his trip to Asia:

Dexter Baker, Air Products and Chemicals Inc.
Winston Chen, Solectron Corp.
Beverly Dolan, Textron Inc.
Robert Galvin, Motorola Inc.
Joseph Gorman, TRW Inc.
Maurice Greenberg, American International Corp.
Bronce Henderson, Detroit Center Tool
James Herr, Herr Foods Inc.
Lee Iacocca, Chrysler Corp.
Robert Maricich, American of Martinsville
Raymond Marlow, Marlow Industries
John Marous, Westinghouse Electric Corp.
Harold Poling, Ford Motor Co.
Heinz Prechter, ASC Inc.
John Reilly, Tenneco Automotive
James Robinson III, American Express
David Roderick, USX Corp.
C.J. Silas, Phillips Petroleum Co.
Robert Stempel, GM Corp.
Michael von Clemm, Merrill Lynch & Co.
Patrick Ward, Caltex Petroleum Corp.

the big three auto manufacturers and other large firms. We went to Australia, Singapore, South Korea, and Japan.

I've had the honor of meeting other U.S. presidents too, and mostly that's because of either NFIB or the Snack Food Association. You may wonder what this has to do with building a business, but I am always energized by being around people who are more influential and more knowledgeable than I am. Also, you never know when you can be a blessing to someone, even if you think they are "above" you.

During the time I was working a lot in the NFIB Washington office I got invited to various business events, and one stands out in my memory. You may remember that in 1991, Russia was big in business news because the Soviet Union had recently collapsed and Russia was transitioning from a government-controlled economy to a private enterprise system. When President Boris Yeltsin was in Washington, I was invited to spend a few minutes with him, representing NFIB. I got to communicate with him my belief that small business is the backbone of a healthy modern economy, and that whatever he could do to promote entrepreneurship would help Russia.

～○～

A friendly discussion is as stimulating as the sparks that fly when iron strikes iron.

Proverbs 27:17

～○～

It's disappointing that there was so much corruption in Russia that small business people never really had a chance to thrive. It reinforced in my mind the need to keep our country a land of opportunity for the average citizen. I say all this to encourage you to use whatever opportunities you are given to help keep our country strong. You may think I'm naïve, but I take literally the verse in Proverbs 22:29 that says, "Do you know a hard-working man? He shall be successful and stand before kings!"

Herr advises Yeltsin

Promote growth, businessman urges

By CHRISTOPHER BIONDI
Staff Writer

WEST NOTTINGHAM — Jim Herr, chairman and chief executive officer of Herr Foods Inc., was among a dozen businessmen who met with Russian President Boris Yeltsin during this week's Washington summit.

Secretary of Commerce Barbara Franklin invited Herr to the meeting and to witness the signing of several accords by presidents Bush and Yeltsin, including one that aims to cut nuclear arsenals by two-thirds.

"It was certainly a momentous occasion because of the fact that instead of spending a lot of money fighting, we are spending it to get a free enterprise system working in Russia," said Herr in an interview.

Before the signing, Herr — also chairman of the National Federation of Independent Business — had an opportunity to discuss business with Yeltsin at a 45-minute meeting organized by the Commerce Department.

"I suggested to (Yeltsin) that if he wants to help the free enterprise system to grow, he needs to allow regulations and laws that would promote growth," said Herr.

"(Yeltin's) overall response to all of us was that they are working frantically trying to have laws enacted to make it possible for growth in the business world," he said.

Among Yeltsin's missions here was to urge Congress to pass a $24 billion aid package Bush has proposed.

"I think President Bush is suggesting a modest amount of help and is hoping that Congress will pass legislation to have that come about," said Herr. "I think it's the right thing to do. We can't go

See HERR, Page A8

From Daily Local News, 06/20/92

73

I got hooked on the book of Proverbs in 1980, through the ministry of a person named Bill Gothard, who was holding conferences in many cities across the U.S. Several members of our family attended a session in Baltimore and Gothard challenged the 3,000 or so of us in the audience to read some of the Word of God every day. He suggested the book of Proverbs, because with its 31 chapters you can read one chapter per day. He said that we would find new thoughts each time we read it, and I found this to be true.

My personal favorite chapter is the eighth day of the month—chapter 8. In that chapter Wisdom says, "I give good advice and common sense." After reading that a few times, I asked God, "How can I take Wisdom along to work?" The very next day, in chapter 9, two verses stood out. Verses 10 and 11 say, "For the reverence and fear of God are basic to all wisdom. Knowing God results in every other kind of understanding. I, Wisdom, will make the hours of your day more profitable and the years of your life more fruitful." I began to see that by giving reverence to God, you are taking Wisdom to work.

I got an idea that we could tie the book of Proverbs into our leadership of Herr's as a source of strength to the company and to others. I began to strategize about how to include Proverbs in our business and the idea came to me that we could print and distribute copies to customers and friends as a gift from our company. Then I thought, "Who could be more helped by the wisdom in Proverbs than the leaders of our country?" so I began to dream of sending each person in Congress a copy.

I talked with Clair Leaman—a friend who had a graphic design and commercial printing firm—about the idea, and he agreed to help me. We contacted Tyndale House Publishers, the copyright holder for the *Living Psalms and Proverbs* and they gave us permission to print and bind our own copies. Clair came up with the idea of calling it "Chips of Wisdom." I wrote an introductory message encouraging readers to take its message to heart. To download the Chips of Wisdom, go to: herrs.com/chipsofwisdomapp or scan one of the QR codes for your electronic device.

iTunes

Google Play

We sent copies to President Reagan and his cabinet and to each member of Congress, and we received 114 letters back from them. I prayed that this little book, that has so much truth in it, would help someone at some decision point in our government to look to God for wisdom. I believe that if the leaders of our country will look to God for wisdom, He will guide them as they create legislation, and our country can remain a land of opportunity for everyone.

Business Principles

Use whatever opportunities you have to be a blessing to others—wherever they are in your sphere of influence.

Work to promote a healthy free enterprise system in our country.

∽◦∽

The good influence of godly citizens causes a city to prosper, but the moral decay of the wicked drives it downhill.

Proverbs 11:11

Chapter 7

MOVING FORWARD

I've always felt that a company that stands still will eventually go backward. You always want to grow and expand your horizons.

Overall, the 1950s were a time of expansion for our industry and for Herr's, but we sure had some setbacks along the way. In the spring of 1952 there was a potato shortage, which if you think about it is devastating to a potato chip manufacturer! The price of potatoes spiked to three times their normal cost because of unfavorable weather conditions.

I talked with my friend Si Musser from Charles Chips and we agreed that I would borrow a truck and drive to North Carolina, where we would purchase potatoes at $7.00 a bag. I would buy 375 hundred-pound bags and we would split them. Well, by the time I got back to Pennsylvania, the price had dropped to $5.00 a bag, but Si kept his word and paid me the price we had agreed upon. We didn't have a written contract, and he could have backed out of our agreement, but he was a man of his word. This reinforced to me that one of the keys to long-term success is keeping your word.

I had a chance to put that into practice for myself a short while later. One August I had visited a Lancaster County potato grower, Morris Nissley, and agreed to purchase $10,000 worth of his crop. As soon as I returned home it began to rain and it rained for two weeks, causing the potatoes I had purchased to develop a jelly rot. I took them anyway and placed them in our plant's storage cellar with the idea that they were still usable. They weren't. We had to haul them out with a manure spreader.

∽⚬∾

The Lord demands fairness in every business deal.
He established this principle.
Proverbs 16:11

∽⚬∾

At the time I wasn't sure how I would get the $10,000 together to pay the farmer. I told him I could pay off the amount $1,000 a year from our profits. Within days a man in the lumber business randomly stopped by to say he wanted to purchase some of the trees on our land. He paid me several thousand dollars for them. Shortly after that, someone wanted to purchase a building lot, and before long I had the whole $10,000. We paid for the potatoes from the sale of assets I had not even considered.

∽⚬∾

Don't withhold repayment of your debts.
Don't say "some other time," if you can pay now.
Proverbs 3:27, 28

In October of 1954, Mother Nature dealt us another blow, with a deadly category 3 hurricane. The employees had gone home for the day and I was in the plant when the storm lifted a portion of our new roof and a steel column shifted and fell, knocking me against a concrete loading platform and breaking several ribs. Moments later, a piece of the steel column landed on my ankle and broke it. Terrified, I managed to crawl beside a cooker, the largest piece of equipment nearby, for protection.

Hurricane Hazel, 1954

When it was all over, I painfully limped across the yard to our home, which thankfully had withstood the strong winds. However, the building nearby that we used for a warehouse was completely flattened and many of our vehicles were destroyed.

❦

Disaster strikes like a cyclone and the wicked are whirled away.
But the good man has a strong anchor.
Proverbs 10:25

❦

The 1950s were full of blessings, too. Our second son, Edwin Hershey ("Ed"), was born April 19, 1955. With three young children at home, Mim's role in the business became more focused on being my confidante and supporter, rather than going to the plant or office each day. She has always been indispensable to me—giving good insights and wisdom whenever decisions need to be made, and always offering the listening ear in times of difficulty or dilemma.

Mim is also a very hospitable person, and since our home is adjacent to the plant, some of our key business associates would come over to the house for dinner with us in the evening. They didn't seem to mind the bedlam caused by our little children, or the simplicity of our meals. They knew we were genuinely glad to get to know them personally.

We began to plan parties at Christmas and in the summer for our employees and their spouses. We feel it's important for employees to enjoy interacting when they're not on the job too, and the company could provide some socials for them. Christmas soon outgrew our dining room table and we rented a room at a nearby restaurant. Eventually we began bringing in some sort of entertainment, such as a musical group or a comedian. The summer event, which we now call the "Summer Social," was always held in our backyard and it is still held on the campus of the business (close to our backyard). Everyone brings their children and we have tents set up with games and clowns and music in addition to the barbeque.

One of our major business decisions came up in 1958: Should we add seasoning to our chips? Today that seems like such a "given"—we have all kinds of new flavors and we advertise our product as a way to "live life with flavor." But back then, it was a new concept and we had to be careful. Would consumers get confused about what

Ira L. and Mary Stauffer Herr,
parents of James Stauffer Herr

Isaac and Esther Burkhart Hershey, parents of Miriam Esther Hershey

James Stauffer Herr
born August 6th, 1924

Miriam Esther Hershey
born November 29th, 1926

"Summer Social" in Jim and Mim's backyard

"Herr's Potato Chips" were? Would they be willing to buy something different? Would it cut into our regular sales?

Our competitors began to try it, and we saw there was some consumer demand, so we began to produce a barbeque flavored potato chip. It became very successful, so we next developed a sour cream and onion chip. Our Old Bay™ seasoned chips were suggested by an employee, since that is a popular flavor in the Chesapeake Bay area. Another popular one was our Salt and Vinegar chip.

To this day we try new flavors. Some of them are winners; others get taken off the market. We try not to have so many products that a store's limited shelf space is overloaded. Ideas for seasoned chips are given to our Research and Development people, and we have a review system to test the flavors and develop new packaging for them. It's a real art to get the right mix of products on the shelf of a retail store.

Our family expanded as our third son, Herbert Eugene ("Gene") was born July 17, 1957, and our second daughter, Martha Jane, was born October 12, 1959. Our five children have all grown up in the business, so to speak. Living across the lawn from the factory, they interacted with the employees (probably to our embarrassment if we knew all that they said or did!), they worked at odd jobs such as sweeping out the truck bays in the evenings or mowing the lawn, and they worked in the plant itself as they became old enough. Our family didn't separate work from everyday living—it was all part of our daily lives, regardless of the time of day. Many business events or decisions were discussed at mealtime.

By 1961, we had 26 employees and a weekly payroll of $2,000. We had 10 routes that covered a radius of about 50 miles. Our mantra then was the same as it is today: to provide quality products at a competitive price and to back up the products with honesty, integrity, and dependable service.

By that time we had begun using our Direct Store Delivery (DSD) system to distribute other products along with the ones we manufactured. We wanted to be a full-service snack company, so that retailers would be less inclined to bring in other vendors who might also sell them chips. We sold salted nuts, dried meat sticks, pretzels, crackers, popcorn, cookies, and, on occasion, my mother's homemade chocolates.

Now there was a product that no one else could match! My mother, who was a good cook, decided to set up a small business of her own, on the top floor of their Willow Street garage (the same location that we had used after the fire). She specialized in making chocolate